A *cool* drink of
WATER

by Barbara Kerley

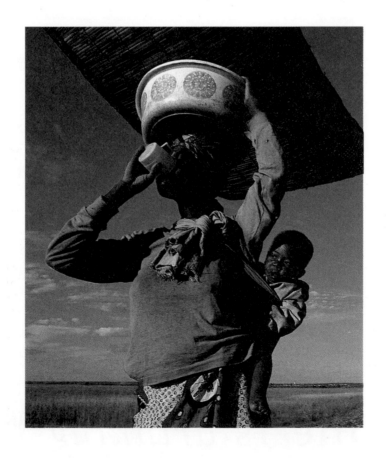

SCHOLASTIC INC.
New York Toronto London Auckland
Sydney New Delhi Hong Kong

Somewhere, right now someone is *drinking* WATER...

Scooped from the **RIVER**

Drawn from a **WELL**

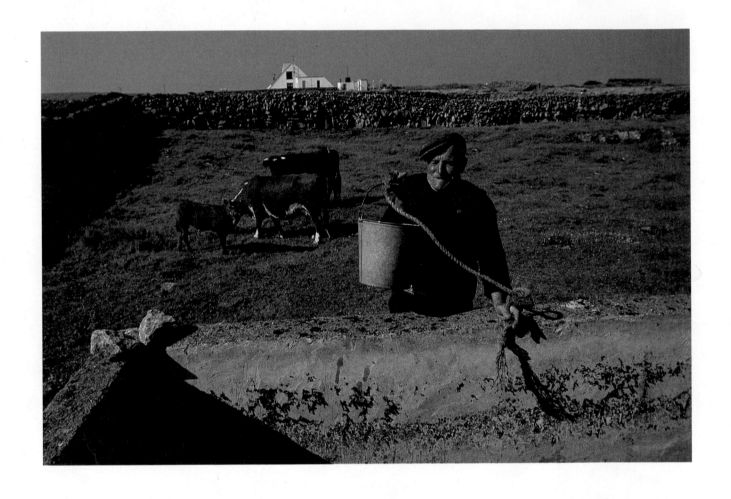

Caught as it *drips* from the **ROOF**

From **FOUNTAINS**

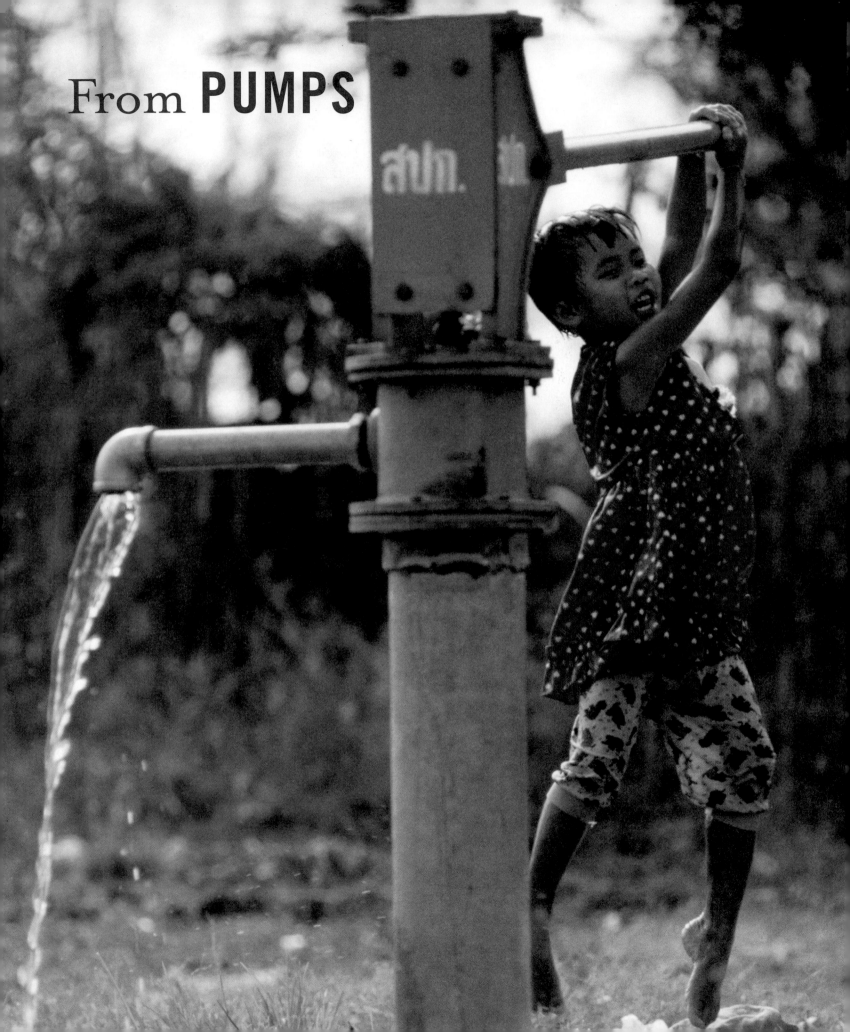

From **PUMPS**

Straight from the **TAP**

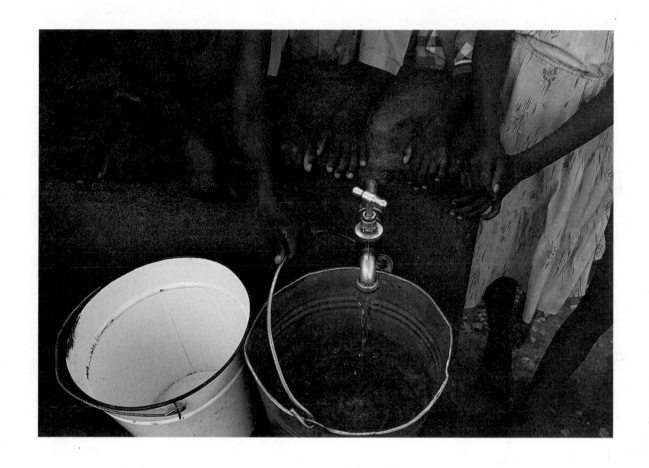

A cool drink of **WATER**

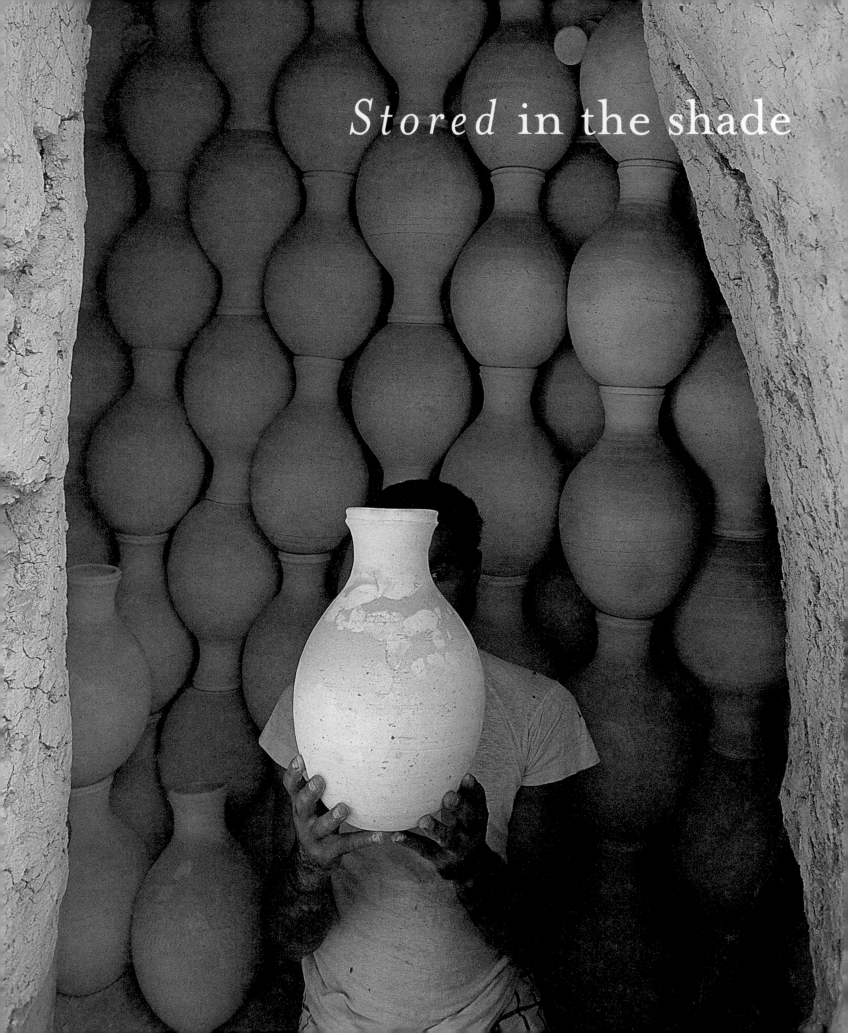

Stored in the shade

in cool, clay **POTS**

Chilled in a **PITCHER** of ice

In **BUCKETS**

Brass **POTS**

Plastic **JUGS**

Caravan **CANS**

A cool drink of **WATER**

Squeezed from a **BOTTLE**

A burlap **BAG**

Sipped from a thin tin **CUP**

Shared in a **FAMILY**

Shared with a **FRIEND**

A cool drink of **WATER**

Everyone

Everywhere

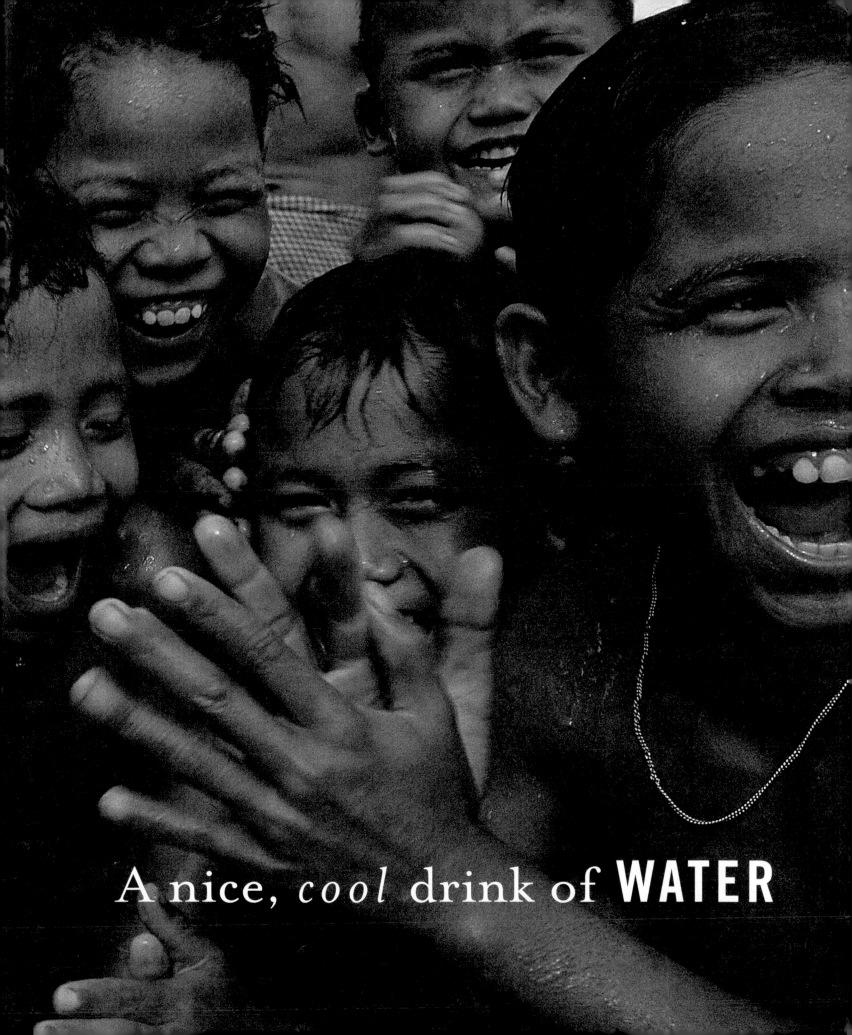

A nice, *cool* drink of **WATER**

A *cool* drink around the WORLD

Arctic Ocean

NORTH AMERICA
CANADA

Rocky Mountains
Skookum Gulch, Oregon
Arizona-Utah Border
U.S.
Des Moines, Iowa
Takoma Park, Maryland
St. Petersburg, Florida

Aran Islands, Galway, Ireland
EUROPE
Monaco
Rome, Italy

ASIA
Thar Desert, India
Pokhara, Nepal
Lugu Lake, Yunnan Province, China
Iraq or Kuwait
Agra, India
Nile River, Egypt
Bahlah, Oman
Gujarat State, India
Fachi, Niger
AFRICA
Prey Char, Cambodia
Phai Sali, Thailand
Tidore Island, Indonesia

Atlantic Ocean

Pacific Ocean

SOUTH AMERICA
Cuzco, Peru

Zambezi River, Zambia

Kanye, Botswana

Indian Ocean

Pacific Ocean

AUSTRALIA
Simpson Desert, Australia

ANTARCTICA

0   3000 miles
0   4000 kilometers

TIDORE ISLAND, INDONESIA
Front cover: Meeting his reflection in a pool of water, a thirsty boy leans over for a welcome sip. In Indonesia's tropical rain forests, rainfall can be as high as 120 inches per year, making water plentiful for all. PHOTOGRAPH BY BRUCE DALE

ROCKY MOUNTAINS, CANADA
Water running off a glacier provides frosty refreshment for a hiker standing on a layer of ice. Melting snow and ice flow from these mountains to the lakes and rivers below. PHOTOGRAPH BY MARIA STENZEL

ARAN ISLANDS, GALWAY, IRELAND
His face ruddy from years of outdoor chores, a man hauls up water for himself and his cows. The well collects fresh groundwater from beneath the island's soil. PHOTOGRAPH BY ANNA SUSAN POST

ROME, ITALY
A young child holds on tight, so that a cool drink doesn't become a cold bath. Built in 1623, the Fontana della Barcaccia (Fountain of a Boat) remains a popular spot on a sunny day. PHOTOGRAPH BY BROOKS WALKER

ZAMBEZI RIVER, ZAMBIA
Toting a basket of fish on her head and a baby on her back, a mother takes a quick water break as she walks down the road. PHOTOGRAPH BY CHRIS JOHNS

AGRA, INDIA
In a practice older than the Taj Mahal itself, a boy scoops water from the Yamuna River. India is home to one-sixth of the world's population, and its many rivers help supply water to its people. PHOTOGRAPH BY STEVE MCCURRY

POKHARA, NEPAL
Sheltered under the roof to stay dry, a boy fills his water jug. During the summer monsoon, or rainy season, rainwater flows easily from the metal roof into a gutter pipe. PHOTOGRAPH BY STEVE MCCURRY

PHAI SALI, THAILAND
Feet lifted clear off the ground, a young girl pulls her weight when it comes to pumping water. Pulling down on the pump handle forces water out the spigot. PHOTOGRAPH BY ROBERT MAASS/CORBIS

KANYE, BOTSWANA

The community water tap is a place for friends to gather and share the day's news before bringing home the family's water. With desert covering more than 80 percent of the country, water taps, fed by underground wells, are essential. PHOTOGRAPH BY PETER ESSICK

GUJARAT STATE, INDIA

Arms held out for balance, two women carry stacks of brass water pots on their heads. They may walk as far as a mile from a well back to their desert camp. PHOTOGRAPH BY DILIP MEHTA

SIMPSON DESERT, AUSTRALIA

A ringer, or cowboy, drinks the old-fashioned way: from a burlap bag. Water is scarce at the Anna Creek Cattle Station, where the average yearly rainfall is a mere 5½ inches. PHOTOGRAPH BY MEDFORD TAYLOR

PREY CHAR, CAMBODIA

Dripping wet in celebration, kids cheer the completion of the town's first water well. Before the well was built, residents relied on a small, muddy pond for all their water. PHOTOGRAPH BY ANNIE GRIFFITHS BELT

BAHLAH, OMAN

Towering overhead, stacks of new clay pots are ready to store water. In these deserts, water is so scarce that the local word for rain is *hayat*, or "life." Oman relies on desalination, which removes salt from seawater, for part of its drinking water. PHOTOGRAPH BY JAMES L. STANFIELD

DES MOINES, IOWA, U.S.A.

Gallons of water are lined up, ready to distribute to residents of Des Moines. In 1993 floodwater from the Mississippi River affected the city's water treatment system, making household water unsafe to drink. PHOTOGRAPH BY JODI COBB

SKOOKUM GULCH, OREGON, U.S.A.

Back warmed by the sun, an old man sips water in Skookum Gulch, in the Klamath Mountains. To live a long and healthy life, a person needs to drink up to eight glasses of water a day. PHOTOGRAPH BY BRUCE DALE

MONACO

Pocket money can buy a bottle of water any time, night or day. The need for clean, plentiful drinking water is something people all around the world have in common. PHOTOGRAPH BY JODI COBB

TAKOMA PARK, MARYLAND, U.S.A.

As beautiful as the centerpiece of a still-life painting, a pitcher of ice water sits on an outdoor table in Takoma Park. Ice cubes, although common in the United States, are a luxury in much of the world. PHOTOGRAPH BY DANIEL SHERMAN

SIMPSON DESERT, AUSTRALIA

A camel caravan walks across a dried salt lake, where years sometimes pass between rainfalls. Carrying water in plastic jerry cans is a necessary precaution when crossing the desert. PHOTOGRAPH BY MEDFORD TAYLOR

THAR DESERT, INDIA

Careful not to spill a drop, a mother drips water from a silver rattle into her baby's mouth. In this arid land, water is so precious that drawing from the well is a sacred act. PHOTOGRAPH BY GEORG GERSTER

NEAR CUZCO, PERU

Girls wait in line to wash up and get a quick drink at their school's new water tap. During the Inca Empire, canals were built in Cuzco to channel the Huatanay and Tullumayo Rivers. PHOTOGRAPH BY CAROLINE PENN/CORBIS

LUGU LAKE, YUNNAN PROVINCE, CHINA

A wooden yoke helps a woman shoulder a heavy load while hauling water from Lugu Lake. With water weighing more than eight pounds a gallon, two full buckets can tip the scales at 40 pounds. PHOTOGRAPH BY MICHAEL YAMASHITA

ARIZONA-UTAH BORDER, U.S.A.

Seated in a swirl of sand and stone, a hiker in Upper Water Holes Canyon drinks water to keep his body hydrated. Water makes up nearly 70 percent of the human body. PHOTOGRAPH BY BILL HATCHER

SOMEWHERE IN KUWAIT OR IRAQ

A victim of the heat and confusion of the 1991 Persian Gulf War, a lost horse accepts a cool drink. Soot from dynamited oil wells poisoned the area's water and air. PHOTOGRAPH BY STEVE MCCURRY

ST. PETERSBURG, FLORIDA, U.S.A.

Back cover: With a splash and a smile, two kids at a park in St. Petersburg enjoy a nice, cool drink of water. PHOTOGRAPH BY CURTIS GRAHAM/CORBIS

A note on *water* CONSERVATION

EARTH HAS BEEN CALLED THE "WATERY PLANET" BECAUSE nearly three-quarters of its surface is covered by precious, life-sustaining water. Yet of that water, 97 percent is undrinkable salt water. Of the three percent that is fresh water, more than two-thirds is caught up in glaciers and polar ice sheets. Humans, animals, and plants survive on less than one percent of the world's volume of water. That's the equivalent of just over a tablespoonful from a gallon jug. In the past, this much water has always been enough. In fact, the amount of water on Earth and these proportions of salt water to fresh water have not changed since the days of the dinosaurs.

> We *live* by the grace of **WATER.**
>
> —NATIONAL GEOGRAPHIC, November 1993

Unlike oil or coal, water is a renewable resource: It recycles itself. Water from the ocean evaporates into the air, gets held in special atmospheric holding tanks known as clouds, and falls to Earth in the form of rain. This rain replenishes lakes, rivers, and groundwater, the main sources for human water consumption.

We humans need water. Nearly 70 percent of the human body is made up of water. We need to drink water regularly—about eight glasses a day is ideal—in order to live. We can survive without food for several weeks, but without water, a human will usually die in less than a week.

Today, our world's supply of fresh, clean water is in danger. But if there's no less water on Earth than there's ever been, then why is this so? In November 1993, the NATIONAL GEOGRAPHIC magazine published a special issue on water in North America. In that issue, William Graves, the editor of the magazine at the time, wrote, "The problem is simply people—our increasing numbers and our flagrant abuse of one of our most precious, and limited, resources." As our population grows and as industry grows, our need for fresh water increases. At the same time, we are shrinking the supply of drinking water by polluting it.

With a dwindling clean supply and skyrocketing demand, our world is facing a serious water problem. Even now, health problems resulting from the use of impure water threaten the world's population, especially in developing countries. By 2025, the United Nations predicts two-thirds of the world's people will face water shortages. Geography also plays a role in water supply. People don't always live near drinking water sources, and transporting water can be very expensive. Of course you'd expect that water would have to be brought to the desert, but even in New York City, water is transported via aqueduct from one hundred miles away.

WATER FOR SALE: *The commercialization of water is a trend likely to continue as clean, fresh drinking water becomes scarcer and scarcer as a natural resource.*

> Filthy *water* **CANNOT** be washed.
>
> —WEST AFRICAN PROVERB

> When the well's *dry*, we know the **WORTH** of water.
>
> —BENJAMIN FRANKLIN, 1746

> *Water* is the best of **ALL** things.
>
> —PINDAR, CA 476 B.C.

What can we do to solve the world's water problems before it's too late? How can we ensure a future where everyone has enough to drink? This work needs to be done on many levels. Both governments and individuals are responsible.

As part of the National Geographic Society's commitment to oceans, river systems, and watershed conservation, we have developed several initiatives to raise public awareness of these issues. These initiatives include Sustainable Seas Expeditions—a five-year project of deep-ocean exploration and public education in the National Marine Sanctuaries—and the Reefs at Risk Program. A new Rivers Initiative helps educate people about rivers and watersheds that they depend on for drinking water and for recreation. The Society continues to fund projects on water-related research through the Committee for Research and Exploration. National Geographic will continue to explore new opportunities to educate the public about water conservation. Maybe someday science and technology will help solve the problem of water scarcity. For example, finding an inexpensive way to remove salt from ocean water would make vast amounts of water available to drink.

For now, however, there's no better way to protect our planet's water supply than to use less water. This is called conservation. It begins in the home with those who have access to plenty of water, and you can help. In the United States we use water at about twice the rate of other industrialized nations. The bulk of U.S. water usage goes toward agriculture—about 70 percent to 80 percent. But at home, approximately 74 percent of our water usage is in the bathroom. The amount of water we use there easily can be reduced with only a little thought. For example, turn off the water faucet while brushing your teeth. Consider installing low-flow shower-heads and toilets. You can even save bathwater in buckets to water the garden: This so-called graywater is fine for plants. When many of us work together in even small ways, we can make a big difference.

By protecting our water supply and using it wisely, we can ensure that now and in the future everyone, everywhere can always enjoy a cool drink of water.

JOHN M. FAHEY, JR.
PRESIDENT AND CEO
NATIONAL GEOGRAPHIC SOCIETY

For my **MOM,** fearless scholar;
and **DAD,** who would have liked this book.

Scholastic is constantly working to lessen the environmental impact of our manufacturing processes.
To view our industry-leading paper procurement policy, visit www.scholastic.com/paperpolicy.

The text of this book is set in Mrs. Eaves and Trade Gothic.
Book design by Melissa Brown.

Text copyright © 2002 by Barbara Kerley.
All rights reserved. Published by Scholastic Inc., 557 Broadway, New York, NY 10012,
by arrangement with National Geographic Society.
Printed in the U.S.A.

ISBN-13: 978-0-545-49669-8
ISBN-10: 0-545-49669-1

13 14 15   40   21 20 19 18 17